SEALS

CONTENTS

*First published in
the United States in 1991 by*
Gloucester Press
387 Park Avenue South
New York NY 10016

Design Rob Hillier, Andy Wilkinson
Editor Fiona Robertson
Photo Research Cecilia Weston-Baker
Illustrations Ron Hayward Associates

Printed in Belgium

Library of Congress Cataloging-in-Publication Data

Bright, Michael.
    Seals / Michael Bright.
        p. cm. -- (Project wildlife)
    Includes index.
    Summary: Describes the different species of seals, their
environments and behavior, and shows how hunting and other
human activities threaten their continued existence.
    ISBN 0-531-17263-5
    1. Seals (Animals)--Juvenile literature. [1. Seals (Animals)]
I. Title. II. Series.
QL 737.P64B75   1991
599.74'5--dc20   90-44925
                                                          CIP
                                                           AC

SEALS

Michael Bright

Gloucester Press

New York : London : Toronto : Sydney

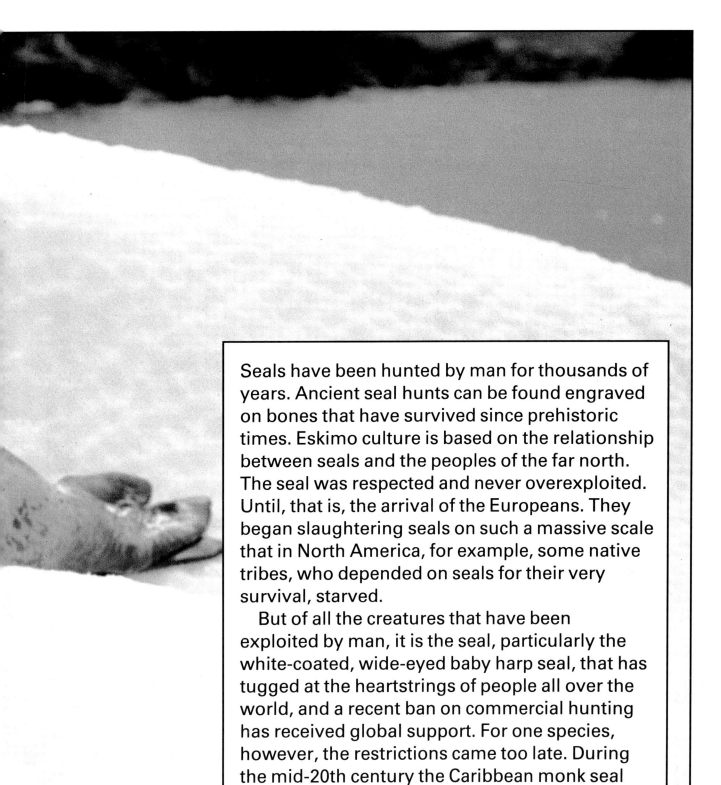

Seals have been hunted by man for thousands of years. Ancient seal hunts can be found engraved on bones that have survived since prehistoric times. Eskimo culture is based on the relationship between seals and the peoples of the far north. The seal was respected and never overexploited. Until, that is, the arrival of the Europeans. They began slaughtering seals on such a massive scale that in North America, for example, some native tribes, who depended on seals for their very survival, starved.

But of all the creatures that have been exploited by man, it is the seal, particularly the white-coated, wide-eyed baby harp seal, that has tugged at the heartstrings of people all over the world, and a recent ban on commercial hunting has received global support. For one species, however, the restrictions came too late. During the mid-20th century the Caribbean monk seal disappeared from the coves and beaches of the West Indies. The last individual was seen in 1952.

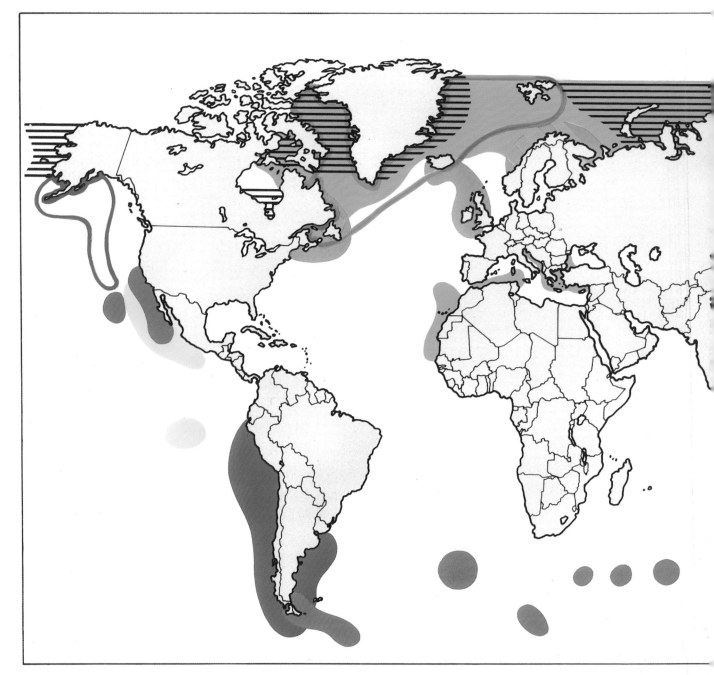

- Elephant Seal
- Hooded Seal
- Harp Seal
- Weddell Seal
- Leopard Seal
- Southern Sea lion
- California Sea lion
- Northern Fur Seal
- Walrus
- Gray seal
- Monk Seal

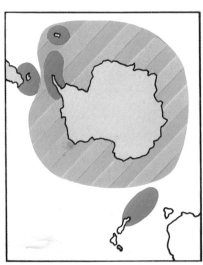

△ The map shows the distribution of some of the seal species that have been hunted commercially. There are many others whose numbers have declined rapidly due to hunting.

◁ In 1786 there were 2.5 million northern fur seals. By 1911, there were 200,000. Numbers rose to 300,000 in 1977 after a regulated cull.

Seal distribution

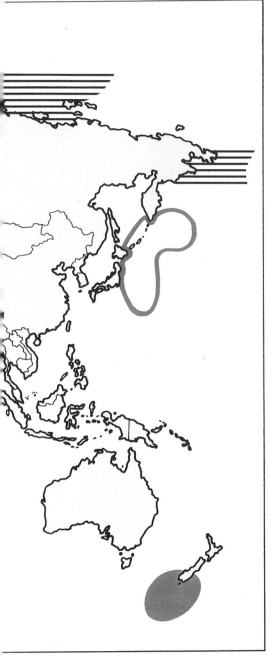

Seals are found in the parts of the world where there is sufficient food, such as the nutrient-rich polar seas. There are, however, some species, such as the monk seals and sea lions, which breed in subtropical and tropical regions, where abundant food is brought up from the depths to the surface in "upwellings." These occur where the cold Humboldt Current sweeps northward along the Pacific coast of South America, bringing nutrients from the Antarctic. Off the coast of Mauritania, fish-rich shallow waters not only provide abundant food for seabirds and waders during the winter, but also for the very rare Mediterranean monk seal.

One way of plotting seal distribution is to track their predators. Seal breeding colonies are not only the focus for adult seals, but also for great white sharks. These enormous sharks have a liking for young seals. Almost all seal colonies in temperate or subtropical seas are visited by great whites. Curiously, great whites also frequent the Atlantic coast of North America, particularly around Long Island and New England. This suggests that there were once seals breeding on these coasts. Now however, these seals have been wiped out.

Hunting seals

When primitive man reached the coast, he began to hunt seals. Seals were considered big enough to be worth killing, as they provided a tribe with several meals, and yet were small enough not to fight back. In those prehistoric times hunters killed only enough for food and clothing.

However, in the 18th and 19th centuries all that changed. Seal hunting became a profitable sideline to whaling, with the seal pelts being made into fur coats. Death for the seals was cruel. They were clubbed, speared or skinned alive. Population numbers plummeted, and the sealers were forced to travel far and wide in search of new seal colonies. One by one the populations were wiped out. The Juan Fernandez fur seal, for example, numbered over 3 million in 1792. Between 1778 and 1805, three million were killed and by 1807, there were only 300 seals left.

> "The commercial seal hunt should be prohibited on the grounds that it causes unnecessary suffering to many seals... and no one can prevent cruelty taking place."
>
> **Trevor Scott — World Society for the Protection of Animals.**

▽ Baseball bats are used in the Pribilof Islands to kill northern fur seals. Until recently, about 30,000 young males were killed each year, despite a decline in pup births.

The killing of baby harp seals on the ice off Newfoundland (the Front herd), and in the Gulf of St. Lawrence (the Gulf herd), has been the most emotive seal slaughter to be brought to world attention. Historically, the early settlers were unable to fish in the winter and so began killing seals for food, leather and oil. Later a market was discovered for the harp seal's fine fur. In two centuries over 70 million harp seals were killed, perhaps the longest and most heartless slaughter of modern times.

By the 1960s, the hunt concentrated on the white harp seal pups. After the hunters had passed, mother seals returned to the mutilated carcasses. In 1983, the European Community banned the importation of baby seal products and the hunting effectively ceased. In 1988, Canada banned the killing of baby seals.

"I never thought I would have to face pictures of horror again. After so many campaigns, it is as if we have regressed into an era of barbarism."

Brigitte Bardot, actress and anti-fur campaigner, on learning about the cull of harp seals in the White Sea in May 1990.

▽ Seal skins being stretched and dried in an eskimo village. For the northern peoples, the seal has been an essential resource, providing meat, oil, clothing, footwear, harpoon lines, and tools.

The trade

The white fur coat of the newly-born harp seal pup proved to be the cause of its downfall. The soft fur became a favorite among the fur trade. Sealers first clubbed the seal pups over the head, and then deftly removed the skin and blubber, known as the sculp, with a knife. In 1928, the crew of the *Bonaventure* killed and skinned 8,000 pups in just a few hours. About 700,000 pelts were taken each year. In the 1960s the furs were commercially traded as "fun fur."

▷ Worldwide, less people are wearing furs. Yet seal fur coats (right) are still considered by some to be luxurious status symbols.

▽ Traditional seal skin boots have a shaft of soft ringed seal leather and a sole made from the tough, durable leather of the bearded seal.

With the restrictions on trade in elephant ivory, some hunters are killing walruses for their tusks. The killing is disguised as a subsistence hunt, but it is not regulated. The tusks are being traded for drugs and alcohol. Conservationists report hundreds of headless walruses being washed up on the remote northern shores of Alaska. Each carcass has a bullet hole in it.

Oil produced from the blubber of seals was originally used in oil lamps, and then later in the manufacture of margarines, lipstick, soaps, and high quality lubricants. The meat was canned and distributed as pet food. Northern and southern elephant seals were slaughtered primarily for the vast quantities of oil obtained from each carcass. Walruses were killed for ivory. Steller's sea lions were killed for their stiff 16in-long whiskers. They were used to clean opium pipes.

In the 1800s a way was found to remove the long, tough guard hairs on a seal skin. This left the soft underfur which could then be made into fur coats and other fur products. This breakthrough marked the rapid decline in fur seal populations. Large seal colonies were almost wiped out in only three or four years as the demand for their skins rapidly increased.

There is another side to seal hunting and trade in seal products. After populations of harp and hooded seals crashed because of overhunting in the mid-19th and 20th centuries, the herds were carefully managed. This means that today there are enough seals to sustain an annual hunt. But the European Community ban on trade in seal products means that the sealers, especially those in the far north who depend on the seal hunt, have lost a large part of their livelihood.

Poisons in the food

One of the greatest threats to seals today is marine pollution. Of all the poisons we have been pouring into the sea, polychlorinated biphenyls (PCBs) have been causing the gravest concern. PCBs have been used since 1929 in the manufacture of electrical goods. PCB production peaked in the 1970s, but today their use is limited because they are known to affect living things. For example, seals in the Baltic Sea, where wastes cannot be flushed out by the tide, and in the southern part of the North Sea, where the heavily polluted rivers of northern Europe pour forth their lethal chemical cocktails, are showing horrifying malformations of their bodies that are thought to be caused by PCBs.

There are about 1.3 million tons of PCBs in the world. Twenty percent is in the oceans, ten percent is locked in the soil, and seventy percent still being used in old electrical components or in garbage dumps. If that latter amount of PCBs was allowed to leak into the sea, scientists believe that many marine animals, including seals, would become extinct.

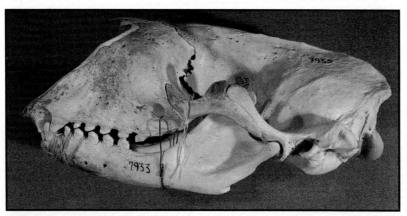

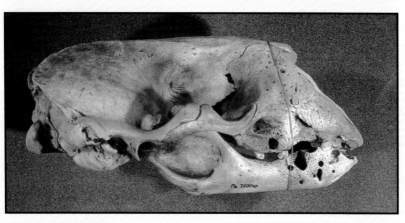

◁ Comparisons between healthy and malformed seals in the Baltic Sea has disturbed marine biologists. The difference between the skull of a healthy seal (shown left) and the skull from a seal which was thought to have been affected by dangerous PCBs (shown below left) is striking.

◁ Apart from damage to the skull (left) seals have been found with parts of their jaws missing, their gums bleeding, or their claws falling off. Inside the body, cancers have been found on several vital organs. Female seals have malformations of their reproductive tract which means they cannot have pups.

Some species of seals, such as the gray and harbor seals, live in close proximity to man and suffer the consequences of man-made wastes. In the North Sea, seals feed on fish contaminated with the chemicals that have been flushed down major rivers, such as the Rhine, from industrial complexes further inland. Many poisonous chemicals are contaminating the marine food chain. Analysis of liver tissue from seals on the German coast show high levels of mercury.

△ Contamination by PCBs is so bad in some parts of the oceans that fish (above) might be considered dangerous to eat. Levels of PCBs in marine mammals, such as seals, built up fourfold between 1969 and 1984. If the current levels continue, seals will be designated as "toxic wastes" by the year 2005.

Habitat pollution

Despite careful management, the population of northern fur seals on the Pribilof Islands has been declining at a rate of four percent each year. Since 1984, commercial killing has ceased, and only subsistence killing is now allowed. Yet the numbers continue to decline. And while it is thought that overfishing of local fish stocks, oil and chemical pollution, and natural disease are taking their toll, marine "litter" is considered to be mainly responsible for the decline.

In the 1950s there was an increase in the use of plastics, resulting in cheaper fishing lines and nets. Unfortunately, if the nets break loose they do not degrade, but continue to drift in the ocean for decades – a process known as "ghost fishing." Seals are caught and drowned in these nets.

▽ A northern fur seal (below) is entangled in a fishing net. To avoid predators, seals often hide in kelp and poke their head through the strands. They do the same with fishing nets. One percent of seals on the shore have nets around their necks. These nets cut into the seal's flesh causing deep wounds which may become seriously infected. With about two thousand tons of fishing gear being discarded in the seas each year, this is thought to be the main factor in the decline of the Pribilof's fur seals.

When an oil tanker runs aground on rocks and the oil tanks are ruptured, or an irresponsible tanker captain washes out his tanks with seawater, or an oil-drilling rig blows out, or an unthinking motorist pours his waste motor oil down the drain, seals and seal lions inevitably suffer. Seals must come to the shore in order to breed or molt, and it is in these coastal waters that they are most at risk from oil pollution. Some seals are not killed by the oil itself but are affected by the chemicals used to clean up the oil spill. And oiled pups tend to suffer from well-meaning animal lovers who try to clean them. Seal experts believe that the disturbance caused by handling and washing the pups can be more damaging than the oil itself.

In the North Sea other types of pollution may affect seals. There has been an increase in the number of young seals found with wounds around the vulnerable navel region. These may be caused by broken glass. Normally salt water would disinfect them, but seals in the Wadden Sea off the coast of the Netherlands, often have high levels of pollution in their bodies which may reduce their resistance to infection.

△ This dead gray seal (above) is covered with crude oil. The thick and viscous oil may have impaired its ability to swim and prevented it from hunting, and so eventually it would have starved to death.

Seals are not often poisoned by oil because they do not clean their fur in the same way that seabirds preen their feathers. Fur seals, however, suffer heat loss when their fur is clogged with oil.

Disease and disturbance

Weakened by the effects of pollution, bad weather, disturbance, overfishing, overcrowding, and blooms of poisonous plankton that destroyed fish stocks, seals in the North Sea succumbed to a highly contagious viral disease similar to distemper in dogs. It was first noticed in April 1988 on Anholt in the central Kattegat, between Sweden and Denmark, and quickly spread, especially during the reproductive and molting periods in the summer.

Soon after the start of the outbreak 18,000 seals had died. The cause of the disease was a mystery. And it was not the first time such a catastrophe had happened. In 1955 and 1980, 400 seals along the New England coast of America and 2,500 Antarctic crabeater seals respectively died from pneumonia associated with an influenza virus. It was thought the virus was carried between distant groups by seabirds.

▽ Baby common seals (below) on Northern European coasts are disturbed by low-flying aircraft and boat traffic. Similarly, the shores of the Mediterranean are crowded with pleasure boats, water skiiers and noisy bathers during the summer. And in the middle of it all monk seals are trying to find a quiet corner where they can meet, mate, and pup. Now they are restricted to remote caves. But, as tourism in the region expands it cannot be long before these sites are also invaded and the seals prevented from breeding. Today the monk seal is one of the twelve most endangered species in the world.

Seals and fishermen are constantly coming into conflict. In some areas, commercial fisheries have fished out stocks and deprived seals of food. Intense fishing by large-scale fishing fleets in the North Pacific is thought to be contributing to the decline in numbers of northern fur seals.

In some places, however, fishermen are claiming the opposite, accusing the rising seal populations of taking too many fish. Whenever such a conflict arises, it is the seals who invariably suffer. But a healthy seal population may be of some benefit to fishermen. Fish are the main predators of fish eggs. If seals take a proportion of the fish predators (mainly noncommercial species) then more eggs will survive to grow up into adult fish and be available for the fishing fleets.

△ Another dead seal is washed up on the beach and taken for examination. All over the world outbreaks of mystery diseases in seal populations are an indication of increasingly unhealthy seas.

"If the seal can't survive in the Mediterranean, then man himself may not be able to. Seals are indicators of pollution, a guide to man's survival."

Keith Ronald, Dean of Biology, University of Guelph.

Protective measures

In the 1980s public opinion was influenced by the propaganda released by animal welfare groups and the media. Pictures of the bloody cull of harp seals on the Canadian east coast, and the slaughter with baseball bats of northern fur seals on the Pribilof Islands, led to worldwide changes in the protection laws for seals.

In Britain, the Prime Minister was deluged by 30,000 letters, received a petition signed by three million people, and met a delegation of trade unionists all demanding a ban on seal killing.

A Gallup poll revealed that 80 percent of British people were concerned for the plight of seals. The same was true throughout Europe, and a ban on baby seal products imposed by the European Community has restricted the slaughter. In 1983, for example, a planned cull of 183,000 harp seals, half of them pups, was banned. The EC ban saved the pups.

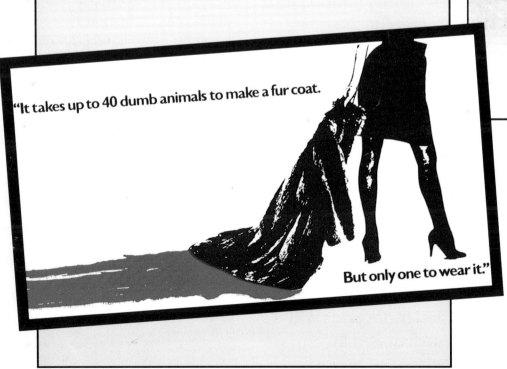

"It takes up to 40 dumb animals to make a fur coat.

But only one to wear it."

◁ This image was used by the British animal rights group, LYNX, in their anti-fur campaign. However, despite similar campaigns worldwide, trade in furs in the United States for example, has tripled over the past decade to a $2 billion industry.

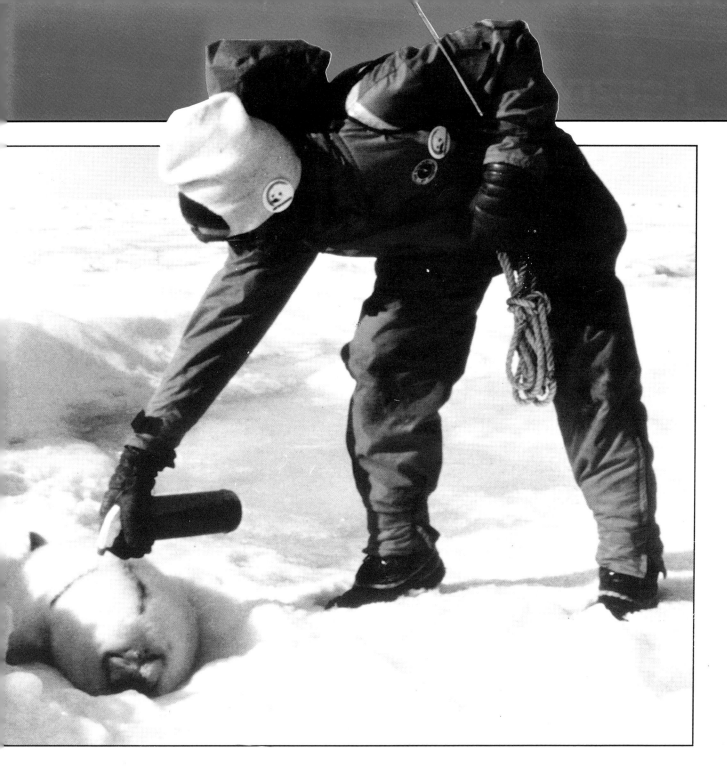

Many species of seals are now protected from hunting, although subsistence hunting is allowed. In some countries, such as Norway, seals can be shot during a limited open season. But the major Norwegian hunt for harp and hooded seals on the ice of the Barents Sea and the White Sea has declined considerably from 69,000 in 1982 to less than 500 in 1986. Also, some killing continues where fisherman believe that seals are eating depleted fish stocks.

△ Before the ban on killing baby harp seals, conservation groups like Greenpeace (above) would venture onto the ice and spray the pups' fur with a dye. In this way the pelt was rendered worthless. Feelings on the killing grounds ran high, as conservationists came into conflict with angry sealers.

Reserves

Some populations of seals were on the brink of extinction during the 19th century, but today most are protected and those that breed in colonies often haul ashore in the comparative safety of nature reserves. The northern elephant seal population was reduced in 1890 to less than 100 individuals in a single herd on Guadalupe Island. Protection given by the Mexican and American governments enabled this population to recover and spread to former breeding sites on the Pacific coast of North America.

▽ These two elephant seals on San Miguel Island are protected. They were born in Channel Islands National Park on the west coast, near California. A large population of seals hauls out at the Ano Nuevo State Reserve, where tourists visiting between December and March can watch the breeding activity.

Monk seals are vulnerable to disturbance from coastal craft and tourists. There are only 500-1,000 Mediterranean monk seals surviving on the coasts of Greece, Turkey, Italy, Cyprus, Morocco, Algeria, Tunisia, and Mauritania. In each country the seals are supposed to be protected, but fishermen still see them as a threat to fisheries, and kill them.

In Greece, however, a reserve has been set up in the northern Sporades in which local fishermen are offered exclusive fishing rights in the nature reserve if they leave the seals alone. Similarly, populations of the very rare Hawaiian monk seal have halved in the past twenty years. The seal therefore is fully protected within the confines of the Hawaiian Islands National Wildlife Refuge. As the seals visit so many outlying islands it is difficult to count them accurately, but it is thought that only 1,400 remain.

△ An increase in tourist traffic to the Pribilof Islands is believed to be contributing to the continuing decline in the numbers of northern fur seals.

Research

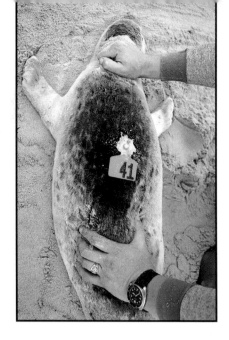

In the Juan Fernandez archipelago off the coast of Chile (where Robinson Crusoe's adventures were based on the real-life marooning of pirate Alexander Selkirk), the fur seals were thought to have become extinct. But in 1965 an expedition found 200 animals hiding in deep caverns. Researchers carefully monitored the colony by tagging pups, counting seals and observing seal behavior. Today the population has increased to over 3,000 seals.

In order to prevent local fishermen from killing the surviving seals, the researchers have introduced an important education program. Their research has shown that the seals do not compete with the fishermen for fish. Instead the seals eat the squid that prey upon the fishermen's main source of survival – lobsters. The education program is aimed at teaching the inhabitants more about seal characteristics and behavior.

△ This common seal is being fitted with a monitor (above) with which scientists can follow its progress.

▽ For large and dangerous seals, monitoring is inappropriate, and so scientists mark animals with numbers and letters (below) that can be seen from some distance away.

Scientists have fitted some seals with equipment that can monitor the depths to which they dive during feeding. They discovered that a female Hooker's sea lion dived repeatedly to 1,400 ft in seas to the south of New Zealand. Weddell seals of the Antarctic go to 1,900 ft. But the champion divers are elephant seals. They descend to over 2,900 ft and spend most of their life deep down when at sea. Researchers believe they can even go to sleep while underwater.

▽ This gray seal is fitted with a transmitter that can be tracked from a satellite in space. In this way scientists can follow the movements of seals and obtain information about their feeding habits and their impact on fish stocks. Already, research has shown that gray seals eat mainly sand eels and not fish caught for human consumption.

The future

The future for many species of seals looks assured. Stocks reduced to very small numbers at the time of the great slaughter in the 18th and 19th centuries have now recovered. But, as man continues to upset the balance of life in the sea with the killing of seals, pollution, or disturbances around seal breeding colonies, even large populations of seals could be endangered.

The killer-disease epidemics that have spread rapidly through the populations of common and gray seals in the North Sea illustrate how vulnerable these animals are. The effects of pollutants on the breeding abilities of seals in the Baltic Sea and in the southern part of the North Sea show that we cannot be complacent about the way we discharge waste chemicals and untreated sewage into the oceans. And, despite long-term research of seal stocks in the Pribilof Islands, the decline in numbers of northern fur seals remains a mystery.

There is no future for the Caribbean monk seal. It is extinct. However, scientists hope that on some remote West Indian island there just might be a few undiscovered survivors.

▽ The Hawaiian monk seal (below) and its relatives in the Mediterranean are very vulnerable. An outbreak of a disease like that which killed many common seals in the North Sea could mark the end of this species.

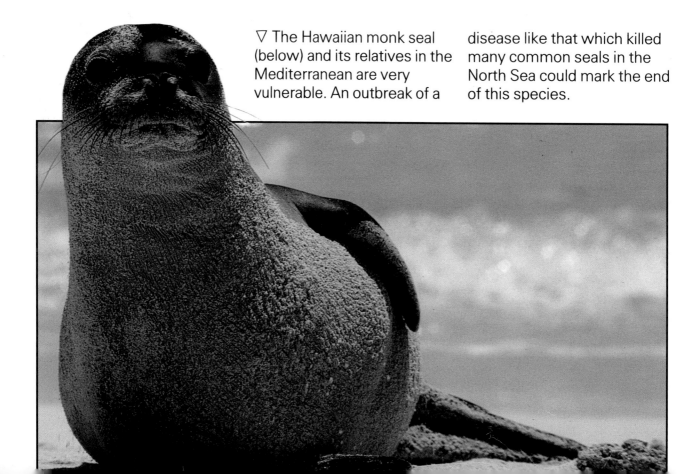

Seals are near the top of their food chain and will be affected by any disturbances in that chain. Seals are also often living in close proximity to man and are directly affected by the way that we treat the sea. If seals suffer in some way and their numbers unexpectedly decline, then this indicates there is something seriously wrong with the state of the oceans. Seals give us an indication about the health of the planet – and there are signs that things are not at all well.

△ Seal pups are safe from the fur traders. Global public pressure has ensured that the killing of white-coated harp seals and blue-backed hooded seals will never happen again. However, the future for this baby gray seal is not so clear. Disease, pollution and culling because of fishing interests mean that the killing continues.

Seal fact file 1

The largest seal is the southern elephant seal. Males are 16 feet long from head to tail and weigh 5,000lbs. Females are smaller at 10 feet and 1,500lbs. The smallest seals are the ringed seal of the Arctic, and the freshwater Baikal seal of Lake Baikal in the Soviet Union. Males and females of both species grow to five feet and weigh 140lbs. The Baikal seal may be a landlocked relative of the ringed seal.

Different types of seal
The true seals are adapted for a life in the sea. They are champion divers and spend long periods underwater. They swim with a sideways movement of the hind quarters. The small forelimbs are used for steering. They must come onto land to pup and move with a rippling movement.

The eared seals, which can be recognized by their scroll-like ears, include the fur seals and the sea lions. They use their foreflippers to propel themselves through the water. On land they are fairly agile as they can use their forelimbs and tail for support. The males of both groups are characterized by a thick shaggy mane.

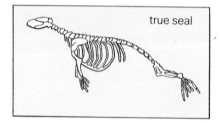
true seal

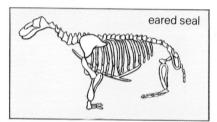
eared seal

Characteristics

About 25 million years ago the eared seals evolved from carnivorous otterlike creatures. The true seals were thought to have evolved separately about 15 million years ago. The modern seal shape is streamlined with no projections to slow progress in water. The head is rounded and tapers into a long neck and then smoothly into the rest of the body. The true seals do not even have external parts to the ears. Teeth vary in size and shape according to the type of food that is caught (see below). Crabeater seals feed almost exclusively on tiny shrimp-like krill. They have small back teeth with special shaped cusps and with few gaps between them. The South American sea lion has teeth that are specialized for grabbing and holding onto wriggling fish, while the Weddell seal has simple teeth.

Hind flipper shape varies with swimming method. Elephant and harbor seals have webbing between "toes" that increases flipper surface. Sea lions, which use foreflippers for swimming, have an extension to each digit and no webbing.

Fur seals have much thicker fur than other seals. Next to the long stiff guard hairs are 50 or more short secondary hairs, whereas in other seals there may be just a few. So fur seals have a thick underfur which is absent in other seals and sea lions.

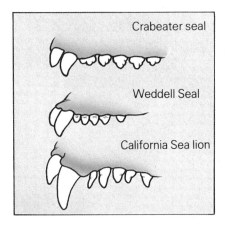

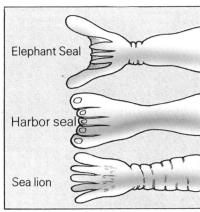

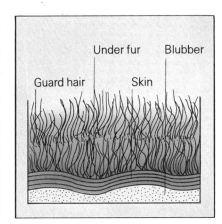

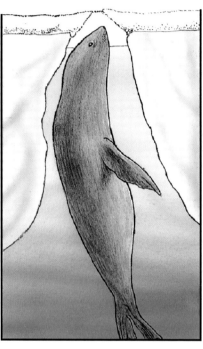

Diving

Eared seals dive for only a few minutes at a time, although Cape fur seals have been known to hunt at 330ft. True seals dive to great depths and stay down for long periods of time. A Weddell seal has been known to dive to 1,400ft and stay down for 73 minutes. To achieve these amazing underwater feats, seals' bodies have many adaptations. Seal blood can carry three times more oxygen than human blood. Seal muscles can also absorb more oxygen than our muscles. In addition, a diving seal's heart rate slows down and blood is diverted away from the kidneys and liver to organs more important during diving, like the brain.

Long dives require a different approach than short dives. Normally a true seal, such as a Weddell seal, will stay under for no more than 20 minutes at a time. In this way it can make numerous dives over a long period of time. If, however, it dives for more than 30 minutes, new rules may apply. When muscles have to go on working after the oxygen supply is used up, as would happen in a long, deep dive, a waste product known as lactic acid begins to accumulate in the muscles. The seal must get rid of lactic acid before it can make its next dive, and this may require a long recovery period at the surface. However, elephant seals can make long dives repeatedly without any recovery periods.

Breathing

Seals obtain all the oxygen they need to make their muscles work before they dive. The deeper they dive the more deep breaths they must take while at the surface. It would be dangerous to dive deep with a lungful of air. The gas would be compressed at depth, the oxygen absorbed and used, but the absorbed nitrogen would remain. As the seal returned to the surface the pressure would get less and bubbles of nitrogen would form in the seal's blood. This is called the "bends" and can be fatal. Seals living below the ice must also maintain breathing holes at which they can gasp a vital breath on returning to the surface (shown above).

Feeding

In order to feed underwater and not drown or swallow too much water, the seal has a special adaptation at the back of its mouth. The tongue pushes against the soft palate and closes off the lungs and throat. Food varies from species to species, but all are carnivorous. The crabeater seal of the Antarctic (right) does not take crabs but eats krill. Walruses and the long-whiskered bearded seals feed on mollusks living at the bottom of the seabed.

Sea lions and leopard seals (right) will eat just about anything that moves including seabirds, particularly penguins. They patrol the sea close to penguin colonies and wait for the birds to return to the water. With a flick of the head, a leopard seal tosses its prey into the air and skins it alive before eating it. Leopard seals also prey upon other, smaller seals. In all species of seals, large fish are broken up with the claws before being swallowed. The teeth are mainly for grasping prey.

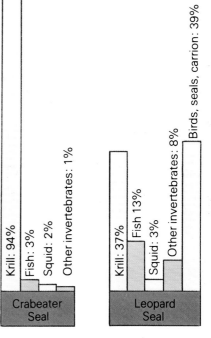

Crabeater Seal: Krill: 94% | Fish: 3% | Squid: 2% | Other invertebrates: 1%

Leopard Seal: Krill: 37% | Fish 13% | Squid: 3% | Other invertebrates: 8% | Birds, seals, carrion: 39%

Voices

Seals are far from quiet creatures. A seal or sea lion rookery is a very noisy place with males snorting, bellowing and belching, and females and pups bleating. Male elephant seals even have an inflatable bulbous nose with which they can make their belchlike calls sound louder. It is used to intimidate rivals and avoid a fight. Some seals also call underwater. Harbor seals (left) click. Male Weddell seals make loud screaming noises under the Antarctic ice. They are declaring their right to a territory. Weddells on either side of Antarctica have different dialects. Male walruses make a sound that resembles somebody striking a loud metallic gong.

Fact file 3

Unlike the whales and dolphins, which give birth to their young in the water, the seals and sea lions have not yet completed the transition from living on land to a life in the sea. So, each year they must haul out onto the land or on ice to give birth.

Courtship and mating

All seals gather at breeding sites, whether in huge, densely packed colonies on a beach or loose assemblies on sand banks, on ice, or in the sea. The bulls arrive first and fight for the right to occupy the best places to attract the females. The cows are sexually receptive a few days or weeks after giving birth.

During mid-winter, groups of 10-15 walrus cows gather at regular breeding sites in the Arctic. When the females haul out on ice to rest, the bulls make a clanging sound, using an inflatable sac in the throat chamber to enhance the sound. The sound display is used to attract the females and entice them into the water to mate.

Territorial behavior

Those bulls that gather a harem of females, such as elephant seals and sea lions, must battle for the right to be "beachmaster" and guard a stretch of shore. They rear up, snort loudly and slam their bodies together (left). The strongest become territory holders and gather as many females as they can acquire. Successful California sea lion bulls gain 16 females each and keep them in a harem for about 27 days, during which time they must remain alert to chase away other bulls. Weddell seals patrol long, narrow, underwater territories that correspond to cracks in the pack ice. The females stay close to the cracks on top of the ice with their pups. The bulls wait below, singing their territorial songs, until the female is ready to mate.

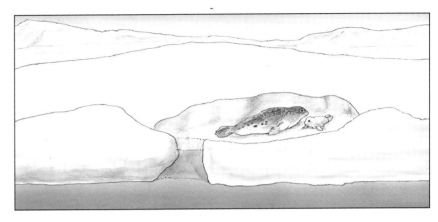

Pupping

Ringed seals in the Arctic give birth to their pups in a snow lair (above) over a breathing hole in fast ice. Harp seals are born in the open on the pack ice (below). Elephant seal pups are born on the beach where they are vulnerable to squashing by the active bulls. Birth is very fast, between one and four minutes, and most pups emerge with a fur coat called the lanugo.

The young

Newborn fur seals have black fur and those pups that are born on the ice have white fur. The hooded seal pups have a blue black coat. The fur is molted after a couple of weeks in true seals and after a couple of months in eared seals. Pups feed on very rich milk and in some species grow rapidly. Weaning can sometimes be unbelievably fast. A hooded seal pup can be weaned in just four days, while the harp seal is not far behind with nine days. The melting of the pack ice during the spring and the chance of being caught out in the open by a polar bear may account for the need for the pup to develop rapidly. Eared seal pups stay with their mothers for much longer, with some taking milk for as long as a year. Weaned elephant seals tend to leave their breeding colony at a time that coincides with a peak in ocean productivity.

Index

Photographic Credits

Cover and pages 13, 15, 20, 22 bottom, 24, 25, 26, 28 and 31: Bruce Coleman Ltd; pages 4-5 and 23: Survival Anglia; pages 7, 8, 19, 21 and 27: Ardea; pages 9, 10 bottom, 16, 17, 22 top and 30: Frank Lane Agency; pages 10 top and 11: Greenpeace Communications; page 12 both: Goran Frisk; pages 14 and 29: Planet Earth Pictures; page 18: Lynx.